Julius Orrin Converse

Garfield, the Ideal Man

Julius Orrin Converse

Garfield, the Ideal Man

ISBN/EAN: 9783337032845

Printed in Europe, USA, Canada, Australia, Japan

Cover: Foto ©Suzi / pixelio.de

More available books at **www.hansebooks.com**

GARFIELD

THE IDEAL MAN.

AN ADDRESS

Delivered before the Geauga County Teachers' Institute, at
Burton, Ohio, Wednesday evening, August 9, 1882,
and the Portage County Teachers' Institute,
at Ravenna, Ohio, Tuesday even-
ing, August 17, 1882.

/BY

J. O. CONVERSE,

Editor of the Geauga Republican, Chardon, Ohio.

CLEVELAND, O.:
WILLIAM W. WILLIAMS,
1882.

GARFIELD, THE IDEAL MAN.

GARFIELD, THE IDEAL MAN.

Mr. President, Ladies and Gentlemen of the Institute, Fellow-citizens:

The life of a truly great man, of world-wide renown, passed into history is a theme which, often as it may be presented can never grow old; and, if that life be one of such noble achievement, and in which centered such high hopes and grand possibilities, as in that of James A. Garfield, forever consecrated and enshrined by martyrdom, it will never cease to be of the deepest and most tender interest. It is as an inexhaustible fountain, from which we may ever draw fresh lessons of wisdom, instruction, and inspiration.

It seems but yesterday since the fatal deed was done which bereft us of that precious life, and, amid the tears of millions, we bore our murdered President to his resting-place at Lake View, and we have scarcely yet emerged from the shadow of that great cloud of sorrow which so suddenly spread like a pall over the Nation; but, as it is slowly passing, we may begin to discern its silver lining, as we trace, though dimly as yet, the outlines of the earthly career of him whose loss we all so deeply deplore.

It is profitable, as well as consoling, now to reflect that great characters and lives, whatever may befall their possessors, are not accidents, nor do great afflictions spring from the ground. To borrow a spray from the departed, who is yet present with us, and who, though dead, yet speaketh, in so many beautiful, comforting, and inspiring words that will live: "It is one of the precious mysteries of sorrow that it finds solace in unselfish thought." Never so "Sweet are the uses of adversity" as when they teach us to find, even in our bereavements and losses, the sources of higher instruction and greater blessing, if we but view them aright. And what is true of individuals is equally true of a Nation. When bowed in grief by some terrible visitation, like the taking off of a Lincoln or a Garfield, it is hard at first to realize how any good can come out of it; but when, in calmer retrospect, we read the lesson of the great martyr's life, we know he has not lived or died in vain, and are lifted up and ennobled thereby.

I approach my theme with diffidence, and touch it only because my heart is full of it. We are yet too near to comprehend its full import. As with great objects in nature, so with great men, it is only in the distance that their grandeur fully appears. "No page of human history," said Garfield, "is so instructive and significant as the record of those early influences which develop the character and direct the lives of eminent men." I can do little more than speak of him as seen from my own standpoint, as his humble friend. What was he? What were the elements of his character? What was the secret of his success? What were the leading motives of his action? What the sources of the majestic current of his great life?

Were I to describe Garfield in a single sentence, as he seemed to me, I would say he was *The Ideal Man*. If, as he believed, "every character is the joint product of nature and nurture," then surely no man was ever more highly favored by these two creative forces. Every man of real, native strength and genuine worth, though he may not measure them, is conscious—and it is no egotism for him thus to be conscious—of the existence of his own peculiar powers as well as weaknesses. He must, to that extent at least, know himself. That Garfield was not wanting in this self-consciousness is evident from his own declaration that, "to every man of great original power, there comes, in early youth, a moment of sudden discovery—of self-recognition—when his own nature is revealed to himself, when he catches, for the first time, a strain of that immortal song to which his own spirit answers, and which becomes thenceforth and forever the inspiration of his life,

"Like noble music unto noble words."

To learn, then, how to estimate the character of a man like Garfield, we should acquaint ourselves as nearly as possible with those elements in him which seem most to be the conscious inner springs of all his thought and action. And in so far as these revealed themselves in his character and life, they proclaimed him what I believe he would have most liked to be regarded, *The Ideal Man.* Not a perfect man, for none are perfect, none without human imperfections and defects; not an *idealist,* in the sense of being a visionary dreamer or Utopian transcendent-alist, for nothing could be more foreign to his nature; but, more accurately speaking, pre-eminently a *man of ideals;* one who, in the grandest and noblest sense, ever strove to make real the ideal in every field of labor, and in every walk of life, from the hum-blest and most obscure to the most exalted and distinguished. From the smallest be-ginning to the culmination of his marvelous career, we find every effort prompted, every achievement gauged and measured, by some lofty ideal. Accordingly, he had no faith in luck, but unbounded faith in patient,

persistent, intelligent industry, which he
expressed in the homely but true proverb,
"A pound of pluck is worth a ton of
luck." "Luck," said he, "is an *ignis fat-
uus*. You may follow it to ruin, but
never to success." And of like import are
these sayings: "Things don't turn up in
this world until somebody turns them up."
"Young men talk of trusting to the spur
of the occasion. That trust is vain. Oc-
casions cannot make spurs. If you expect
to wear spurs, you must win them. If you
wish to use them, you must buckle them
to your own heels before you go into the
fight." "Occasion may be the bugle-call
that summons to battle, but the blast of a
bugle can never make soldiers or win vic-
tories." "Growth is better than perma-
nence, and permanent growth is better than
all." "For the noblest man that lives there
still remains a conflict." "I am more than
ever convinced," said he, in a conver-

sation at my house, but a year or two
before his death, "that, other things being
equal, the great differences between men
are, after all, in their relative capacities for
hard work." In saying, "If you are not
too large for the place, you are too small
for it," he was but expressing in other
words the thought that every man should
ever keep before him some grand ideal, be-
yond his present attainment, in every
sphere of duty and endeavor. With a life
molded and fashioned by such high and
noble conceptions, he was of necessity an
ideal boy, an ideal scholar, an ideal soldier,
an ideal statesman, an ideal friend, husband,
father, MAN. To him even the Presidency,
a prize so many inferior men have vainly
coveted, though the free gift of a great
people, came too soon. "This honor," he
remarked at the Williams Class dinner in
Washington, on the day before his inaugu-
ration, "comes to me unsought. I have

never had the Presidential fever, not even
for a day, nor have I it to-night. I have
no feeling of elation in view of the position
I am called upon to fill. I would thank
God were I to-day a free lance in the House
or the Senate. But it is not to be, and I
will go forward to meet the responsibilities
and discharge the duties that are before me
with all the firmness and ability I can command." But he was not unambitious. He
may have thought of the Presidency as an
honor not to be prematurely grasped, but
to be gratefully accepted when it should
come to him at last, in the fulness of time,
when his labors and triumphs in other fields
should be complete, as the ideal crown of a
well-rounded life of devotion to the public
service. He would have made an ideal
Senator, and to forego his natural desire,
seemingly about to be realized, to enter the
Senatorial arena after graduation from the
House, even with the Presidency in view,

was like missing an essential link in the chain of an ideal ambition. Knowing him, and remembering the early promise of his administration, can we doubt that, had he lived, he would have proved an ideal President?

The scope of a lecture like this will permit but a glance at a few of the many branches of the life of Garfield in which he may be said to have realized in greater or less degree his own ideals. And, first, we will view him as *The Ideal Teacher.* I use this term not in a restricted or technical, but in the broadest and most comprehensive sense, as implying all that is expressed in the terms educator and scholar. We have reason to believe that no other period in this life was so full of interest to him, or regarded by him with so much satisfaction, as that in which he was known only as a scholar or teacher.

Emerson says, in his lecture on "The

American Scholar," that "it is one of those
fables which, out of an unknown antiquity,
convey an unlooked for wisdom, that the
gods, in the beginning, divided man into
men, that he might be more helpful to himself; just as the hand was divided into
fingers, the better to answer its end. The
old fable," he avers, "covers a doctrine ever
new and sublime; that there is one man,—
present to all particular men only partially,
or through one faculty; and that you must
take the whole society to find the whole
man. Man is not a farmer, or a professor,
or an engineer, but he is all. Man is priest,
and scholar, and statesman, and producer,
and soldier. In the divided or social state,
these functions are parceled out to individuals, each of whom aims to do his stint
of the joint work, whilst each other performs
his."

"In this distribution of functions the
scholar is the delegated intellect. In the

right state he is Man Thinking.   In the de-
generate state, when the victim of society,
he tends to become a mere thinker, or,
still worse, the parrot of other men's thinking."

Though some may hesitate to accept
this definition to the fullest extent, all must
admit that, on the whole, Garfield, in the
character of his mental processes, in the
depth and breadth of his culture, and in the
quality and variety of his gifts and achieve-
ments, realized more nearly than any other
man of his time, the Emersonian ideal of
the American scholar — Man Thinking.
When in the maturity of his powers and at
the height of his usefulness and fame, we
could hardly think of him as a scholar, for,
though we recognized his rare acquire-
ments, they seemed never prominent save
as an element in that complete, symmetrical
manhood of which he was so splendid an
embodiment and type.   The most perfect

results are attained only when we are unconscious of the skill or ability in any
particular department they require, and
affected only by their influence. The most
eloquent orator does not impress us with
the thought that he is eloquent, but his
eloquence, like a subtle, all-powerful influence, moves and thrills us, we know not
why. And so of the true scholar. Garfield
was so much more than an ordinary scholar
—so utterly devoid of everything resem-
bling pedantry—that, while he gave us so
abundantly of his unfailing mental re--
sources, we received his gifts, like the air
and light of heaven, unconscious of their
presence.

In seeking for the elements which made
Garfield the Ideal Teacher, let us first inquire how he was regarded by those with
whom he was earliest, longest, and most
intimately associated in the same field
of labor and pursuit,—who drank with

him the earliest and richest draughts from the fountain of knowledge. And here we find but one unvarying testimony: that he was, first and foremost of all, an ideal student. Garfield recognized the fact that he who would govern must first learn to obey; he who would be a successful teacher must prove himself capable and worthy by being a patient, industrious, and faithful pupil. I quote from President Hinsdale's "Hiram College Memorial," as follows:

"President H. W. Everest, of Butler University, Indiana, who was a student with Garfield in Chester, as well as a student and teacher with him in Hiram, thus speaks in a late private communication:

"'I met him first at Chester. Rooming in the same building, and working for a while at the same carpenter's bench, we soon became intimate. He was a noticeable student, both on the play-ground and in the class-room. We recited Robinson's algebra together, and belonged to a literary society of our own getting-up, called the "Mystic Ten." At Hiram I was not classed with him, yet knew much of him as a student, but more of him as a teacher. My estimate is briefly as follows; and for many of the items I remember distinct illustrations:

" ' 1.   His intellections were clear, vigorous, and easy in all directions, but especially so in the languages.

" ' 2.   He did not study merely to *recite* well, but to *know*, and for the pleasure of learning and knowing.

" ' 3.   It was his main object to master the thought, but the language was retained with the thought.

" ' 4.   As study was the easy play of his mind, so to recount and review his lessons and reading was a frequent pleasure.

" ' 5.   He was a master at condensed classifications, so that his memory easily held and reproduced what he had learned.

"'6. He had a wide-awake curiosity, which seemed never to be satiated. A new thing, however unimportant, always attracted his attention.

"'7. He had a great desire and settled purpose to conquer, to master the lesson, to prove superior to every difficulty, to excel all competitors, to conquer and surpass himself.

"'8. With this desire to conquer, there was found the most generous and exultant admiration at the success of another.

"'9. Over all his study he shed the glory of a happy disposition—of youth, hope, and manly courage.'

"All these points," remarks President Hinsdale, "are well taken, but several of them deserve especial emphasis. He studied to *know*, and for the pleasure of learning and knowing. With this may be connected President Everest's seventh point,

Garfield's settled purpose to conquer, to prove superior to every difficulty. His love of victory, over men or things, was the strongest; but it was a love born of the noblest elements. He took no pleasure in a merely personal triumph; but a triumph that was a test of honorable superiority, he keenly enjoyed. Here, too, may be mentioned his full appreciation and generous recognition of all men, even though competitors or opponents. His determination to master whatever he undertook, especially to subdue his own nature, is well illustrated by an anecdote. Sitting on a log in the edge of the woods, back of the college building in Hiram, he once said to the companion of his walk : 'I have made a painful discovery. I have found that my mind needs interest in a subject to incite it to continuous action. The other day I tried to read through a long bill in which I had no interest ; it was merely my duty to

read it. My attention wandered, thus
revealing a defect in my training. If I
cannot otherwise overcome this defect,' he
said, 'I will give up my work, renounce
public life, go to Germany, and take a full
course in one of the universities. I must
be full master of my powers at any cost.'

"At this time he had been in Congress
several years."

Years after Garfield had ceased to teach,
and when he had already acquired a national reputation as a statesman (to further
quote from the same work), he one day
gave a lecture to the teachers' class in
Hiram College, in which he related the following anecdote, characteristic of himself
in this early yet important period of his life:

"When I first taught a district school, I
formed and carried out this plan : After I
had gone to bed at night, I threw back the
bedclothes from one side of the bed. Then
I smoothed out the sheet with my hand.

Next, I mentally constructed on this smooth surface my school-room. First I drew the aisles, here I put the stove, there the teacher's desk, in this place the water-pail and cup, in that the open space at the head of the room. Then I put in the seats, and placed the scholars upon them in their proper order. I said here is John, with Samuel by his side; there Jane and Eliza, and so on, until they were all placed. Then I took them up in order, beginning next my desk, in this manner: This is Johnny Smith. What kind of a boy is he? What is his mind, and what his temper? How is he doing? What is he now as compared with a week ago? Can I do anything more for him? And so I went on from seat to seat, and from pupil to pupil, until I had made the circuit of the room. I found this study and review of my pupils of great benefit to them and to me. Besides, my ideal construction, made on the bed-sheet in the dark, aided me materially in the work."

To President Everest's analysis of Garfield's character as a student, I here add his analysis of his character as a teacher:

"1. He was always clear and certain.

"2. He impressed the main things, but passed perhaps too lightly over the subordinate portions.

"3. He had rare ability at illustration.

"4. He gave more attention to the boy than to the book. He strove to develop the student, not the lesson or science.

"5. He was abundant in praise of success, but sparing of blame.

"6. He inspired his students with a spirit of investigation and conquest.

"7. By frequent and rapid reviews he kept the whole work in hand, and gave it completeness."

Among the peculiar qualifications of Garfield as a teacher, I would name the power

of self-control ; he was ever master of himself. And not the least of his qualifications
was his generous and sensitive appreciation
of the needs and possibilities of those
under his charge—a qualification every
teacher ought to possess, and in which he
was certainly unsurpassed, if not un-
equalled. It was this, joined with other
qualities, that gave him the tact to meet all
emergencies that might arise, and turn them
to the best account for the good of the
individual scholar and the interest of the
school. In the spirit of the ideal teacher,
as well as of the philosopher, patriot, and
philanthropist that he was, he could say in
his address on The Elements of Success:

" I feel a profounder reverence for a boy
than for a man. I never meet a ragged
boy on the street without feeling that I may
owe him a salute, for I know not what possibilities may be buttoned up under his
shabby coat. When I meet you in the full

flush of mature life, I see nearly all there is
of you ; but among these boys are the
great men of the future,—the heroes of the
next generation, the philosophers, the
statesmen, the philanthropists, the great re-
formers and molders of the next age.
Therefore, I say, there is a peculiar charm
to me in the exhibitions of young people
engaged in the business of education."

In estimating Garfield's service in the
cause of education, we are not limited to
that period of his life in which he was
known and recognized merely as a student
or teacher, rich and fruitful as it was in its
wealth of intellectual and moral resources,
—but the same characteristics were mani-
fested alike in the school-room, the pulpit,
and the forum. Since to educate, and be
educated, was to him the business of life,
he was never content with present attain-
ments or old methods, and his constant
plea was for a higher and more practical

education. "The old necessities," he declared, "have passed away. We now have strong and noble languages ; rich in literature, replete with high and earnest thought, the language of religion, science, and liberty; and yet we bid our children feed their spirits on the life of the dead ages, instead of the inspiring life and vigor of our own times. I do not object to classical learning —far from it—but I would not have it exclude the living present." Accordingly, he did not leave his character as a teacher behind him when he entered Congress, but there gave to the country the ripe fruit of his thought and experience as an educator in such exhaustive and unanswerable speeches, and well-matured and beneficent laws, for the promotion of National education, as had never before emanated from the mind and heart of any American statesman. He believed (to use his own words) that "the intellectual resources of this country are the elements that lie behind all material wealth, and make it either a curse or a blessing;" and, so believing, " I insist," said he, "that it should be made an indispensable condition of graduation in every American college [as our legislators are at last coming to regard it as an essential qualification in a school-teacher], that the student must understand the history of this continent since its discovery by Europeans, the origin and history of the United States, its constitution of government, the struggles through which it has passed, and the rights and duties of citizens who are to determine its destiny and share its glory."

Sufficient importance has never been attached to the fact that Garfield was the author of the bill for the establishment of a National Bureau of Education, which became a law in 1867, and, although it met with much unwise opposition, and was subsequently reduced to a bureau in the De-

partment of the Interior, it will stand as a
monument to his far-seeing statesmanship
long after the smaller schemes that now
engross the attention of politicians and
divide the people into parties and factions,
shall have been forgotten. He was also
the author of that section of the Revised
Statutes of the United States which pro-
vides for Army Post Schools,—a measure
from which, if carried out as it should be,
untold benefits may be expected to follow.
Besides being the author of both these
measures, he was a most earnest, persistent,
and eloquent supporter of every scheme
for advancing the just claims upon the Government, of education, science, and religion. "The children of to-day," said Garfield, "will be the architects of our
country's destiny in 1900;" and "school-
houses are less expensive than rebellions."
In his speech in favor of his bill for the
establishment of a National Bureau of Edu-

cation, he made the humiliating statement
that, "if we inquire what has been done
by the Governments of other countries to
support and advance public education, we
are compelled to confess with shame that
every Government in Christendom has
given more intelligent and effective support
to schools than has our own." This he
supported by ample authorities and statis-
tics, showing especially the condition of
education under the leading Governments
of Europe. He stated that "teaching is
one of the regular professions in France;
and the Government· offers prizes, and
bestows honors upon the successful instruc-
tor of children. . . . After a long and
faithful service in his profession, the teacher
is retired on half-pay, and, if broken down
in health, is pensioned for life." Contrast
this with the short-sighted and illiberal
policy too often pursued in this boasted
land of free schools, where, as Garfield

conclusively showed in the speech from
which I quote, an enlightened and generous
policy is more essential than in any other;
for here, to use his own forcible language,
"The alternatives are, not education or no
education; but shall the power of the citizen be directed aright toward industry, liberty, and patriotism? or, under the baneful
influence of false theories and evil influences, shall it lead him continually down-
ward, and work out anarchy and ruin, both
to him and the Government?" "Liberty,"
in the calm, philosophic view of a Garfield,
" can be safe only when suffrage is illumined
by education," for "the life and light of
a Nation are inseparable."

I have only to add of Garfield as the
Ideal Teacher, that he never ceased to be a
student, nor to learn from all sources,
—books, or nature, or men—even the hum-
blest and most obscure.

Early transferred from the school room

and the forum to the field, at the call of his country, which was to him as the voice of God, Garfield could not but make *The Ideal Soldier*. The quality or value of his service in the war for the Union is not to be measured by the period of its duration, though long enough to include Middle Creek, and Shiloh, and Corinth, and Chickamauga; nor by the rank he held, or the numbers he commanded, though, in scarcely more than a year, he was successively Lieutenant-Colonel, Colonel, Brigadier-General, Chief-of-Staff, and Major-General, and though he showed himself a master spirit at a most important and critical period of the conflict; but by the same grand conceptions of the meaning and issues of war and peace that made him elsewhere the ideal teacher and statesman. It was true of our late war, as of no other great conflict in the world's history, that it developed the sublimest courage and devotion in the purest and most peaceful walks of life, and, when it was ended, left fewer traces than any other of like magnitude, of violence and demoralization. As a rule, our soldiers went forth to battle from no love of arms, but from an imperative sense of patriotic duty, and those who survived returned to their homes and their former pursuits, to mingle again with the mass of their countrymen, and prove themselves as worthy and exemplary in peace as they had been loyal and valiant in war. And, in such a conflict, I repeat, Garfield could not but be the ideal soldier. "Ideas," said he, "are the great warriors of the world, and a war that has no ideas behind it is simply brutality." He fitly described his own ideal of a battle when, in his oration on General George H. Thomas, he said of that noble soldier: "To him a battle was neither an earthquake, nor a volcano, nor a chaos of brave men and frantic horses involved in vast explosions of gunpowder. It was rather a calm, rational combination of force against force." "Think," he exclaimed, in addressing the Boys in Blue in New York, during the campaign of 1880, " think of the great elevating spirit of war itself. We gathered the boys from all our farms, and shops, and stores, and schools, and homes, from all over the Republic, and they went forth unknown to fame, but returned enrolled on the roster of immortal heroes." Philosopher as well as soldier, he realized that "after the battle of arms comes the battle of history," and that "victory is worth nothing except for the fruits that are under it, in it, and above it." Of the fruits of such a war as the one in which he drew his sword, he thus eloquently spoke on Decoration Day, May 30th, 1868, at Arlington, where, with thoughts of his country "redeemed, regenerated, and disenthralled," he stood " beside the graves of fifteen thousand men, whose lives were more significant than speech, and whose death was a poem, the music of which can never be sung:" "This arena of rebellion and slavery is a scene of violence and crime no longer. This will be forever the sacred mountain of our capital. Here is our temple; its pavement is the sepulchre of heroic hearts; its dome, the bending heaven; its altar candles, the watching stars." With unwavering faith in the promise of the Right, he could "look forward with joy and hope to the day when our brave people, one in heart, one in their aspirations for freedom and peace, shall see that the darkness through which we have traveled was but a part of that stern but beneficent discipline by which the great Disposer of events has been leading us on to a higher and nobler National life."

Summoned by the voice of the people from the school-room to the service of his

State, and thence by the call of his country to the field of duty and of glory, Garfield was soon recalled to enter upon that more distinguished career of statesmanship which, extending through nearly two decades of almost uninterrupted successes, was to culminate in his promotion to the most exalted station in the gift of any people, and be crowned at last with an immortality of fame. Is it too much to say in this presence, and with his life and martyrdom still fresh in all minds and hearts, that Garfield had earned his right to be called *The Ideal Statesman?* Where else in all our history as a Nation, shall our ideal be realized, if not in him, whose life was so complete and full of meaning? What, then, were the elements in the character of the ideal statesman, that Garfield exemplified in his career? These, namely: He should be a man of broad and liberal culture, honest purpose, catholic spirit, and

untiring industry, thoroughly conversant
with the history, wants, resources, and
possibilities of the country, and the *whole*
country. Loving his country and race, he
should be a patriot in the broadest, best,
and noblest sense, which would make him
a philanthropist as well, and, though of
necessity a strong party man where parties
are representative of great principles and
policies, never giving to party what |was
meant for his country or mankind. To
him ''Partisanship is opinion crystallized,—
party organizations are the scaffoldings
whereon citizens stand while they build up
the wall of their national temple.'' He
should, moreover, be, what the mere poli-
tician unfortunately is not always, a man of
deep, earnest, and abiding convictions upon
all questions vitally affecting the moral welfare of the people, and possessing the courage thereof, to boldly avow them, when to
do so would be to incur the danger of

differing from the majority of his party, or being misunderstood by his friends,—believing that, in the end, "the men who succeed best in public life are those who take the risk of standing by their own convictions." And, finally, as the crowning glory of all, he should be a Christian gentleman. "This public life," wrote Garfield, "is a weary, wearing one, that leaves one but little time for that quiet reflection which is so necessary to keep up a growth and vigor of Christian character. But I hope I have lost none of my desire to be a true man, and keep ever before me the character of the great Nazarene." All these essentials of the ideal statesman were found in Garfield, and it was because he possessed them in such an eminent degree, and so harmoniously blended in his grand and symmetrical character, that smaller men sometimes failed to comprehend, and were even inclined to criticise and disparage

him. The noblest elements of his greatness were at times mistaken for weaknesses.
He was too honorable ever, for the sake of
a temporary advantage, to misstate the
position of an opponent, but, on the con-
trary, he would disarm criticism and give
proof of the consciousness of his own
strength by stating it more fully and accurately than he could do it himself. He would
never compromise the proprieties of debate
or lower the ideal standard of parliament-
ary dignity to win a cheap reputation for
personal courage. If he ever seemed to
modify a statement in debate, it was of his
own position, and not of another's, and
from magnanimity, and not from fear. No
braver soul ever lived. His ideal of states-
man-like courage was the true Shaksperean
one :

> " I dare do all that may become a man;
> Who dares do more is none."

Like the memorable sentiment of Henry

Clay, "I would rather be right than be
President," is this of Garfield: "I would
rather be beaten in Right than succeed in
Wrong." "There are some things," said
he in a speech at Cleveland, "I am afraid
to do; I confess it in this great presence: I
am afraid to do a mean thing." And no
braver or more sublime utterance ever
came from the lips of a Christian statesman
than, when a candidate for the Presidency,
he said at Chautauqua: "I would rather
be defeated than make capital out of my
religion." He could indorse no such motto
as "Everything is fair in politics;" but
public and private honor and virtue were
alike, to him, "dear as the apple of his eye."
I can never forget how, in the conversation
at my house, to which I have before alluded,
he emphasized the necessity of maintaining
the National credit. He said he had often
been reminded, during the contests over the
currency, of the pious exhortation heard at

religious meetings, to stand up for Jesus.
Then, rising with his thought, as he often
would in private conversation, as well as
public speech, and with that peculiar ges-
ture of his strong, uplifted arm, so familiar
to those who knew him, he added: "The
public credit is the Jesus of our political
faith;"—a sentiment as noble as it was
characteristic of this ideal statesman. "Let
us," said he, in a speech on the financial
situation, "have equality of dollars before
the law, so that the trinity of our political
creed shall be equal States, equal men and
equal dollars throughout the Union."

Having profoundly studied the problem
of free government, Garfield well under-
stood all the conditions of our National
existence. He saw that greater liberty
involved greater responsibility to the individual citizen—the unit of power in the
Republic—and that wealth, extension of
territory and increase of population, with-

out corresponding patriotism, intelligence
and virtue, would but augment the perils of
our institutions.   It is not surprising, therefore, that the famous prediction by Macau-
lay, of the ultimate failure of our Constitution, as one " all sail and no anchor,"
should have weighed upon his mind, and
been more than once quoted in his
addresses.   It was to him, as to every
thoughtful American, like an alarm-bell in
the night.   But his unswerving fidelity
alike to his country and his ideal, con-
strained him to answer the great English-
man :   " We point to the fact, that in this
country we have no classes in the British
sense of the word—no impassable barriers
of caste.   Now that slavery is abolished,
we can truly say that through our political
society there run no fixed horizontal strata
through which none can pass upward.   Our
society resembles rather the waves of the
ocean, whose every drop may move freely

among its fellows, and may rise toward the
light until it flashes on the crest of the
highest wave."

The Hon. A. G. Riddle, in his admirable
analysis of Garfield's character and life,
which his great friend declared was to himself "a revelation," written while he was
yet a member of the House, asks and well
answers these among other questions:
"Why don't he lead his party in the
House? Long service, rare ability, complete mastery of all the essentials—position
included—quickness, temper, personal bear-
ing, absence of enmities, all unite. The
reins train carelessly through the hall, are
thrown over his desk repeatedly, are sometimes in his hands, and admirably used on
occasion. Why don't he take them firmly
as his, assert himself, be the man he is, and
make the most of it?" The answer Mr.
Riddle finds in his lack of egoism, or self-
seeking. There is also, in my judgment,

another answer. A man so royally en-
dowed, so richly and variously cultured, so
broad, so magnanimous, so philosophical,
could never be a mere parliamentarian, or
dashing gladiator in the arena of debate; and
accordingly, on the higher plane whereon
he moved so grandly, though an acknowl-
edged leader, he always led the *thought*
rather than the *tactics* of the House, and
this was, to him, an ideal leadership. At
the same time, he gave the most thorough
and careful attention to the minutest de-
tails of every question which came before
Congress. A noteworthy example of this,
as well as of his comprehensive statesmanship, is to be found in the act under which
the census of 1880 was taken, which is sub-
stantially the same as the bill introduced
and advocated by him for the basis of the
census of 1870, and which then passed the
House but failed in the Senate. He
believed that a census should not be a mere

compendium of barren figures, but that it
should exhibit as fully as possible the life,
the progress, and the resources of the people. In a speech in the House, February
18th, 1879, in advocacy of this bill, he said:
" If we had the power to photograph the
American people in one second, all in one
picture, and get all the conditions that the
inquiries of the census could give us all at
once, as through a telephone, and have it
all recorded, it would be the ideal perfect
census."

My theme expands as I go forward, and
I must end as I began. To define in a single sentence all the greatness of Garfield,
he was *The Ideal Man*. Strength, symme-
try, completeness, are words descriptive of
the magnificent structure of his ideal manhood. He was brave, yet considerate and
forbearing; conservative, without weakness
or compromise; ambitious, without selfish-
ness or dishonor. Barring all that was

unworthy, we might apply to him as most fitting, all the eulogium pronounced by Antony upon Brutus:

> " This was the noblest Roman of them all ;
> All the conspirators, save only he,
> Did that they did in envy of great Cæsar ;
> He, only, in a general honest thought,
> And common good of all, made one of them.
> His life was gentle ; and the elements
> So mix'd in him, that Nature might stand up
> And say to all the world, This was a man !"

Living or dying, two things Garfield ever aimed to win and merit: his own self-respect and the smile of God. As he remarked in his speech before the Ohio Legislature accepting his election as Senator, " I have represented for many years a district in Congress whose approbation I greatly desired ; but, though it may seem, perhaps, a little egotistical to say it, I yet desired still more the approbation of one person, and his name is Garfield. He is the only man that I am compelled to sleep with, and eat with, and live with, and die

with; and, if I could not have his approbation, I should have bad companionship."

From his post of duty in the House, he
went to Chicago, all unconscious of what
awaited him, yet seemingly in accordance
with that strange Providence which guided
him ever onward and upward to the end
of his career, to become the ideal candidate of the great party to whose support
he had devoted the best energies of his
manhood, because he believed it to repre-
sent the highest interests of his country
and the welfare of mankind. Here I need
not dwell, for the sequel suggests its own
sad and impressive lessons more forcibly
than any words of mine can express them.
I can only repeat the thoughts that came
welling up from my heart when, as his remains lay in state in our Forest City of
Cleveland, we all stood, overwhelmed and
appalled, in the presence of the Nation's
great sorrow:

*" I look back upon Garfield's wonderful
life; I reflect upon its humble beginnings,
its heroic struggles, its sublime achieve-
ments, its brave, tender, self-denying devotion, its magnificent culmination, and its
sad and tragic ending, and it seems as if
some grand orb, long coursing through the
heavens, had suddenly fallen from the
zenith into the depths of immensity; but
what a track of brightness it has left behind! My mind goes back over the long
and eventful period of his service as our
Representative in Congress, and I remember with what eager interest and just pride
men of both parties among his old constit-
uents received the news of his election to
the Senate, and finally of his nomination
at Chicago; I recall the incidents of that
ever-memorable campaign which followed,
in which he, as its central figure, bore him-

---

* Remarks at the Opera House, Chardon, Ohio, Sunday
evening, September 25, 1881.

self so grandly, speaking often, yet saying
nothing his most critical friends could wish
unsaid, but much that will command the
lasting admiration of the world; I think of
that most beautiful and impressive scene,
at the last reception given him on his way
home from Chicago, and which touched
him more deeply than any other incident
of that triumphal journey, when he was
escorted through our streets, amid the
ringing of bells, the firing of cannon, and
the glad acclaim of the people, and the
children of our public schools turned out to
shower his pathway with flowers; I think,
too, of his modest, feeling, rather sad words
on that occasion, his assurances to near
friends that the honors and trials of the
Presidency were by him unsought, as they
would involve the sacrifice of his home life
for a term of years, after which, though
still in the strength of a vigorous and use-
ful manhood, he would be compelled, in

deference to usage, to retire from public
life, or, to use his own expression, 'be shut
up like a leaf in a book,' and his sincere
and earnest assertion that he cared more to
have the old Nineteenth District stand by
him than to gain the election; I hear his
voice, I see his grand, manly, generous,
kindly face looking full upon me; I feel the
strong, magnetic pressure of his hand, and
then I think of him as the innocent, patient,
heroic victim of the darkest of crimes, and
it quite unmans me.

"There was something unspeakably pa-
thetic in those last days of the stricken
President, when, from his cottage window
by the sea, he looked sadly but hopefully
out, and watched the ships as they passed
upon the waters. Withdrawn, as sooner
or later all must be, from the busy world,
and powerless as a child, this patient, suf-
fering ruler of fifty millions of people felt
in the vastness and grandeur of the ocean

a sympathy with his own great life, whose tide was fast ebbing out into the unknown depths of the infinite and eternal. As he began his career with a strange longing for the sea, it was fitting, if his ardent longing for his Mentor home could not be gratified, that he should be permitted thus to die in sight of its waves, and within the sound of its voice, which well might give one deep, sympathizing moan as his great soul went home to God!"

To Garfield, education was a growth, the endless unfolding of God-given powers; war, a conflict of great and enduring forces; politics, the noble science of government; religion, a life; the end of all sacrifice and endeavor, individual and national character. He lived an ideal life, and, with all the world watching in prayer at his bedside, breathlessly listening to catch the last pulsation of that heart which never beat but in sympathy with all that is loyal and good and true, he died an ideal death. Though foully stricken from the height of his earthly career, he has left his country and the world the rich legacy of a peerless, ideal fame, to which the honors of the Presidency could but give an added lustre, and which time cannot dim.

On the Saturday preceding the final obsequies, and while those precious remains were being borne from Washington to Cleveland, I, in company with a devoted and life-long friend of the dead President, drove to Mentor, being actuated by a desire to visit once more the home where he had welcomed us in life, though the light of his presence had gone out forever. The pictures on the walls, the historic office, the library where we had met one year before, and in fact almost everything else, remained unchanged; but, oh! what a void, that could never be filled! On the sadly-memorable Monday following, in company

with the same friend, after listening to the
services in the Park at Cleveland, I left in
advance of the funeral cortege, and, securing
an entrance inside the lines of sentinels that
guarded both sides of the street, walked sor-
rowfully up Superior street to Erie, thence to
Euclid Avenue, and thence on and on until
we reached Lake View Cemetery,—that
beautiful, ideal burial ground of his choice,—
where, standing in the rain by the side of
the public vault, I saw all that was mortal of
Garfield laid to rest. It was, indeed, a
magnificent pageant, such as I may never
again behold; but, to me, it was all unreal,
for I could not feel that Garfield was there.
That great soul, which made him the ideal
man he was, had returned to God who gave.

www.ingramcontent.com/pod-product-compliance
Lightning Source LLC
Chambersburg PA
CBHW031801090426
42739CB00008B/1105